SO-AUP-180

REAL WORLD MATH FOR THINKING KIDS

Math Museum

Exploring Geometry Through Shapes and Patterns

Published in cooperation with
Children's Discovery Museum of San Jose
San Jose, California

No part of this publication may be reproduced in whole or in part, or stored in a retrieval system, or transmitted in any form or by any means, electronic, mechanical, photocopying, recording, or otherwise, without written permission of the publisher. For information regarding permission, write to Scholastic Inc., Instructional Publishing Group, 555 Broadway, New York, N.Y. 10012.

Copyright © 1995 by Scholastic Inc.   All rights reserved. Published by Scholastic Inc.   Printed in U.S.A.
ISBN 0-590-27894-0
1 2 3 4 5 6 7 8 9 10   09   01 00 99 98 97 96 95 94

We investigate shapes to reveal patterns, structures, and relationships.

Math Museum

We use shapes, patterns, and symmetry to create designs and divide space.

Video

SUBCONCEPT
1

We make two-dimensional and three-dimensional shapes
to represent the world around us.

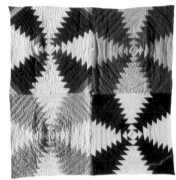

What Shapes Are Around You?

Look around you. Shapes are everywhere. What shapes do these things have?

Sort shapes.

DO·iT
- Take some classroom things. Sort them into groups that show cubes, rectangular prisms, spheres, cylinders, pyramids, and cones.
- Label the groups.

You can use:
- Classroom things
- Paper
- Pencil

SHARE·iT
- Describe the things in each group. What do they have in common?
- Record what the class found out about each group.

BUILD·ON·iT
- Play "Guess My Shape." Think of a shape. Describe it to your partner.
- Ask your partner to guess your shape.

THINK
What things in your classroom have more than one shape?

What Would You Put in a Math Museum?

A museum is a place that shows all kinds of art and interesting objects. But you can find math in a museum, too. You can make shapes for your own math museum.

Artist —
Alexander Calder

You can use:
Geoblocks
Paper
Pencil
Scissors
Tape
Index cards

Make shape sculptures.

DO·IT
• Trace all the faces of a
 geoblock on a sheet of paper.
• Cut out the pieces. Tape them together
 to make a shape sculpture.

SHARE·IT
• Describe the shape sculpture you made.
• How many sides does it have?

BUILD·ON·IT
• Make another shape sculpture
 using two geoblocks.
• Write a description of your
 sculpture for the
 math museum.

THINK

Where is the
rectangle in a
cylinder?

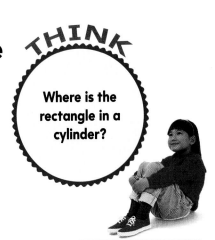

What Shape Pictures Can You Make?

A museum can have sculptures, paintings, and drawings in it. What kinds of shapes can you find in a picture?

Artist —
Kasimir Malevich

Make a shape picture.

You can use:
Pattern blocks
Paper
Crayons or markers
Index cards
Newspapers or magazines

 DO·IT
- Put together pattern blocks to make a picture.
- Trace or draw the picture you made.

 SHARE·IT
- Describe your picture. What shapes did you use?
- How many of each shape did you use?

BUILD·ON·IT
- Cut shapes from newspapers or magazines.
- Then put the shapes together to make a collage.
- Write a description of your collage for the math museum.

Artist —
Aleksandr Rodchenko

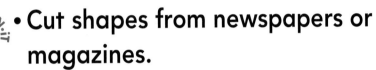

THINK

Why is a square also a rectangle?

9

What Little Shapes Are in Big Shapes?

Sometimes things are not what they seem. You might be surprised to find what shapes are hidden in other shapes.

Find the hidden shapes.

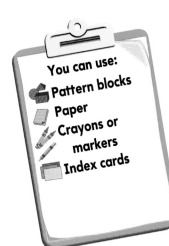

You can use:
Pattern blocks
Paper
Crayons or markers
Index cards

DO·iT

- Make a shape picture with some pattern blocks and trace the shape.
- Trade pictures with a friend. Look for shapes that can fit in your friend's tracing.
- Record the shapes you find.

Shapes We See

6 △

2 ▱

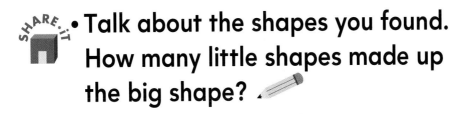 • Talk about the shapes you found. How many little shapes made up the big shape? ✏️

• Draw a large shape. Show what smaller shapes can fit in it.

THINK

What shapes could be hidden in a rectangle?

11

How Can Shapes Tell a Story?

You can use tangrams to tell stories. What characters can you make with tangram pieces? What story would you tell?

Make a tangram picture.

DO·iT • Take some tangram pieces.
Make a picture with them.

• Draw the picture you made.

You can use:
Tangram pieces
Index cards
Paper
Pencil
Calculator

SHARE·iT • Describe the picture you made.
What shapes did you use?

• Tell a number story using the
tangram picture.

BUILD·ON·iT • Use your tangram pieces to make
a storybook character.

• Work with a group. Put your
tangram characters together.
Write some number stories using
your characters.

THINK

How many
squares can you
make with your
tangrams?

How Can You Set Up Your Shape Gallery?

All the projects for your math museum have to do with shapes. How about making a shape gallery for the museum?

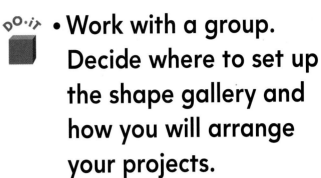

Set up the shape gallery.

You can use:
- Your projects
- Paper
- Pencil

DO·IT
- Work with a group. Decide where to set up the shape gallery and how you will arrange your projects.
- Estimate how much space you will need.

SHARE·IT
- Tell how your group estimated.
- What decisions did you make about arranging the projects?

BUILD·ON·IT
- Describe one project in your shape gallery.

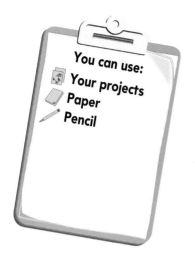

Lupe
I made a collage.
tried to find all
circles.

Ethel
The flower is
growing.

Jim
I made a design.
The biggest shape
was the triangle.

THINK

What is the most common shape in your gallery?

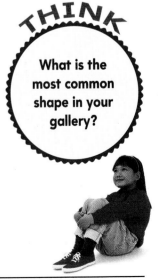

How Can You Make a Repeating Pattern?

Another gallery you can make is a pattern gallery. Some art uses special patterns. What repeating pattern do you see in these designs?

Make a repeating pattern.

DO·IT
- Use pattern blocks. Pick one shape.
- Try to make a repeating pattern with it.

You can use:
- Pattern blocks
- Paper
- Crayons or markers
- Index cards

SHARE·IT
- Talk about how you made your repeating pattern.
- Did you flip or turn the shape to make your pattern?

THINK

Where have you seen repeating patterns?

BUILD·ON·IT
- Make a drawing that shows a repeating pattern.
- Write a description of your drawing for the math museum.

How Many Shapes Can Cover a Floor?

Here are some repeating patterns you can walk on! The patterns on these floors were made with tiles. Which floor has more tiles?

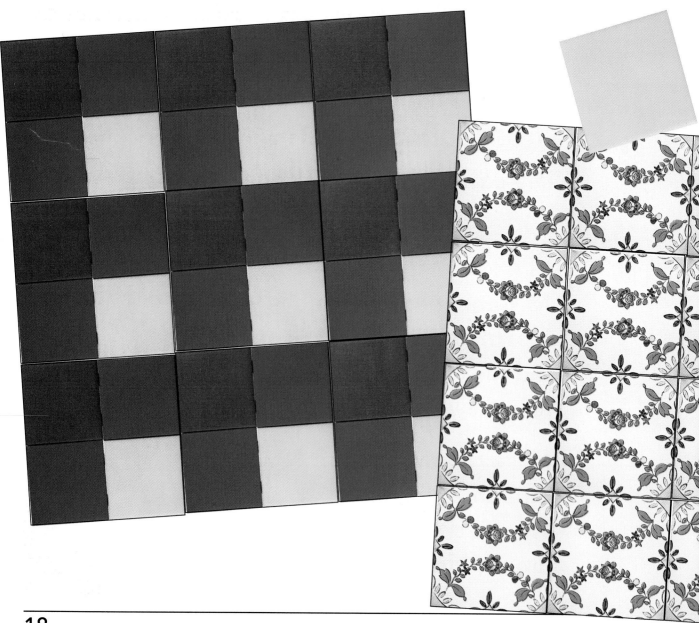

Make a floor pattern.

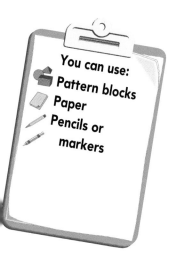

You can use:
Pattern blocks
Paper
Pencils or markers

DO·iT

- Take some pattern block "tiles" and cover a paper "floor" with a repeating pattern.
- Make a drawing of your floor.

SHARE·iT

- Tell what tiles you used. How many did you use?
- Did anyone use a different number of tiles? How were their tiles different?

BUILD·ON·iT

- Are there any gaps in your floor pattern? Estimate how many of your tiles could fill in the gaps.
- Write a description of your floor pattern for your pattern gallery.

THINK

Can you use your tiles to cover a floor that has a different shape? Try it.

What Is Symmetry?

These things in nature and art have symmetry. What do you think symmetry means? What other things have symmetry?

Make symmetry shapes.

DO·IT • Fold a sheet of paper. Start at the folded edge and cut out a shape.

• Unfold the shape. How does it show symmetry?

You can use:
Paper
Scissors
Geoboard

SHARE·IT • Share your shapes. Do any of the shapes show symmetry in more than one way? How do you know?

• Write a description of your own shape for the math museum.

THINK

What letters in your name show symmetry?

BUILD·ON·IT • Make a shape on part of a geoboard. Have a partner make a matching part to show symmetry.

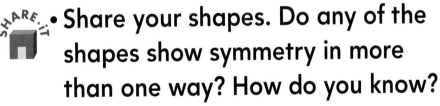

Where Can You Find Equal Parts in Art?

Quilts often have special patterns that show equal parts. What patterns do you see in these quilts? Which one shows equal parts?

You can use:
Paper in different sizes and shapes
Crayons or markers

Show equal parts.

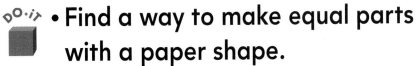

DO·IT
- Find a way to make equal parts with a paper shape.
- How can you be sure the parts are equal?

SHARE·IT
- Tell what shape you started with. How many equal parts did you make?
- What is the shape of each part?

BUILD·ON·IT
- Make color designs with your paper shapes. Color the equal parts in different colors.
- Describe one of your designs.

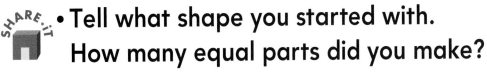

THINK

What things in your classroom show equal parts?

What Can Quilt Halves and Fourths Look Like?

Do you see fourths in these quilts? What about halves? What do $\frac{1}{4}$ and $\frac{1}{2}$ mean?

Make designs showing halves.

DO·IT
- Make a square shape on a geoboard.
- Find different ways to show half a square with a rubber band.
- Fold a paper square to record each of the ways. Color to show $\frac{1}{2}$.

You can use:
- Geoboard
- Rubber bands
- 3" x 3" paper
- Crayons or markers

SHARE·IT
- How many different ways did you show halves?
- What shapes are they?

BUILD·ON·IT
- Use a geoboard. Make designs showing fourths.
- Record the ways on paper squares.
- Color each paper square to show $\frac{1}{4}$.

THINK

Can you show that two fourths make a half? Try it.

25

How Can You Make a Quilt With Your Designs?

Have you ever made a quilt? Some museums have quilts in them. You can add a quilt gallery to your math museum.

Make a quilt.

You can use:
- Your $\frac{1}{2}$ designs
- Your $\frac{1}{4}$ designs
- Tape
- Dot paper
- Pencil

DO·IT
- Put your $\frac{1}{2}$ and $\frac{1}{4}$ designs together to make a quilt. Try it several ways.
- Decide how you want to make the quilt. Then tape your designs together to make it.

SHARE·IT
- Describe how you arranged your designs.
- How many of each design did you use? How many did you use altogether?

BUILD·ON·IT
- Record your design on dot paper.
- Write about the designs in your quilt.

THINK

How would you describe the shape of your quilt?

How Can You Make a Border for Your Quilt?

A border can be plain or fancy. But any border will give your quilt a finished look. How will you put a border on your quilt? Estimate how long your border will be.

Make a border.

You can use:
Paper strips
Scissors
Glue or tape
Paper
Pencil

DO·iT
- Find out how much border you need for your quilt.
- Use paper strips to make the border.

SHARE·iT
- Tell how much border you used.
- Compare the lengths of the borders.

BUILD·ON·iT
- Work with a group. Put your quilts together to make a group quilt.
- Put a border around the group quilt.
- Write about how your group made the border. Also write about how long the border is.

THINK
How long would a border around your classroom be?

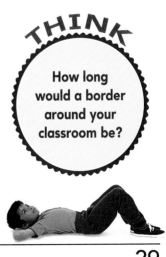

How Much Space Does Your Group Quilt Cover?

Quilts are made in different sizes. They can be as big as people want to make them. How big do you think this quilt is?

Figure out the space.

 • Work with your group to find out how much space your group's quilt covers.

 • Talk about how your group figured out the space.
• Which group's quilt has the longest border? Which covers the most space?

 • With your group, write a description of your quilt.
• Decide where to put your quilt gallery and estimate how big it has to be.
• Hang up the quilts. Do they all fit? What does this say about your estimate?

You can use:
Your group quilt
Paper
Pencil

THINK

How many sheets of paper would cover your desk?

What Can You Tell Others About Your Math Museum?

Make a poster for your math museum. Show the galleries. Describe them.